Don't Curse Your Valley

A 30-Day Christian Devotional

by Renee` Shipp

ISBN- **13: 978-1479265282**
ISBN- **10: 1479265284**

DEDICATION

This book is dedicated to all of us who have gotten to the place in our walk with God where we find ourselves asking, "Why do I have to go through this," or "What did I do wrong to end up here," or maybe we've just said, "I just want to hurry up and get through this!

ACKNOWLEDGMENTS

My most sincere gratitude must go to my Lord for this urgent message He gave me for myself and for His Church.

I also want to thank my husband, Lawton, for his patience during those evening and early morning hours as I sat with a laptop in my lap, writing.

Thank you to Mrs. Becky Dykes, for helping me to make the cover "pop!"

And a very special "Thank you" to Ms. Beth Rogers of *Around the Loop Publications* for her help and expertise in the finalizing of this work.

I also want to thank all of you who read the early copy of this devotional and encouraged me that this, my first Christian book, really does make sense.

PREFACE

Epilepsy again; great depression to the point of uncontrollable weeping; couldn't seem to remember what I was doing even from one moment to another because of several back-to-back brain seizures; falling to pieces over very small things; Great humiliation as a high school teacher, because I couldn't remember student names even after teaching them for several months; sinking deeper and deeper into hopelessness. Great negative emotions; overwhelming depression. Humbled, but thankful to have my husband, Lawton, take me to and from work because of the brain seizures. I felt myself curling up inside, wanting to just go home and stay there; to hide out, I guess; trying to escape from everything. What in the world was happening to me and WHY?

However, at the altar at my church one Wednesday night in February of 2015, I heard the Holy Spirit say to me, "Stop Cursing This Valley!" It looks like He would have pitied me and babied me and said everything was going to be okay; that I had had more than my share of heartaches and disappointments in my life. But this was such a real Word. I knew it was Him and I told God okay.

He told me not to be afraid of my valley but to open my eyes (spiritually) and look at it – to take a look at everything in that valley, but not to be afraid. Then I heard Him ask me to give up everything; my sons, my job, along with any hope for another, any ministry desires and any hope for change – all of it. And I did.

Since then, a cloud that I didn't even know was there, a cloud of depression, anxiety and fear has been lifted. He said I should just stop cursing my valley and rest in my relationship with Him until I was able to walk out of it, which would happen only with His help and on His timetable. This devotional developed as a result of that encounter with the Lord and has seriously impacted my life.

This is not defeat; this is not weakness; this was then and still is complete and total trust in God and His will not only for my life, but the lives of those that God wants to reach through me.

TABLE OF CONTENTS
Daily Readings

QUOTATIONS

"Faith isn't always the ability to move mountains; faith is the ability to keep trusting God when the mountain doesn't move."

Jeff Scurlock, Pastor
First Assembly of God
East Brewton, Alabama

Don't Curse Your Valley

DAY 1: DON'T CURSE YOUR VALLEY!

Psalm 23:4 *(KJV)*
4 Yea, though I walk through the valley of the shadow of death, I will fear no evil: for thou art with me; thy rod and thy staff they comfort me.

When I heard the Holy Spirit say to me, "Don't Curse Your Valley!" I knew it was Him; I knew His Voice, but it startled me. It seems to me that as I was going through one of the toughest times of my life, my Comforter, the Holy Spirit would have held me close, tenderly letting me know that He was with me; that He would have said, "I've got you, Renee; I will help you through this tough time in your life." Instead, that oh-so-familiar Voice said, "Don't Curse Your Valley!"

There was no condemnation in His Voice; It was full of love and understanding. But it was also full of a tremendous amount of expectation; as if God were saying, "I know what I've invested in you over the past several years; I've given you everything you need to get through previous valleys and if something is still needful to enable you to get through this one, I will supply that as well. Stop cursing this valley!"

PRAYER: Lord Jesus, the place I find myself in today is so hard – seemingly impossible. But Lord, I choose to respond to Your request of me to 'stop cursing this valley.' I don't know what today or tomorrow holds, but I know, Lord, that You are in control. So I choose right now to receive Your peace, knowing that Your great Love for me is quite enough to keep me together during this difficult time. I love You, Lord; I really do.

A Moment of Personal Reflection . . . .

How deep is your valley? Have you, like me, found yourself complaining about how difficult and unfair life is right now? What do you hear God telling you about your valley and how you should respond to it?

_____

_____

_____

_____

_____

_____

_____

_____

_____

_____

John 10:3 _(KJV)_
3 To him (the shepherd) the porter openeth; and the sheep hear his voice: and he calleth his own sheep by name, and leadeth them out.

DAY 2: YOU ASKED FOR IT!

Isaiah 55:9 (KJV)
9 For as the heavens are higher than the earth, so are my ways higher than your ways, and my thoughts than your thoughts.

At some time during this heavy, hard-to-figure-out thing in my life, I heard the Holy Spirit say to me, "Renee, you asked for this valley!" I thought that either I was going crazy, or God was about to lay a strong Word on me.

He began to show me times when I wept and prayed, asking and even begging Him to use me, to heal me, to show me anything in my heart that was not pleasing to Him and to clean it up! I wanted so much for God to use me as a vessel to pour His Presence into others' lives – and of course, He knew that.

So He answered me with a valley – an extremely difficult place where I would be emptied of myself and filled with Him. Sounds awesome, right? I honestly did not know what I was asking for!!!

Have you ever looked into the eyes of someone who did not know God and hurt for them, knowing the peace they could have if they would only seek Him? Have you ever asked or even begged God to use you? Be careful what you ask for. You just might get it!

PRAYER: Lord, I had NO idea what I was asking for when I asked, and even *begged* You to use me; but I am so glad I did! Help me, Lord, as I walk with You, to trust You and Your Will for my life – even for today. I still want You to use me, Lord, I really do.

6

A Moment of Personal Reflection . . . .

What if it's true! What if your own desire to serve the Lord and to be a real witness to His life-changing power before others is the *very reason* why you are in your own personal valley? Would you take back your request to God to be such a witness? Or did you really, really mean it? Because if you did mean it, then your life *will count* in the Kingdom of God more than you can imagine. Write your own prayer here of your acceptance of this valley – by faith. You will be glad you did!

_____

_____

_____

_____

_____

_____

Psalm 40:3 *(KJV)*
3 And he hath put a new song in my mouth, even praise unto our God: many shall see it, and fear, and shall trust in the LORD.

DAY 3: *THEY* DID THIS TO ME!

Matthew 6:12-15 (KJV)

12 And forgive us our debts, as we forgive our debtors. 13 And lead us not into temptation, but deliver us from evil: For thine is the kingdom, and the power, and the glory, forever. Amen. 14 For if ye forgive men their trespasses, your heavenly Father will also forgive you: 15 But if ye forgive not men their trespasses, neither will your Father forgive your trespasses.

You may realize that this particular valley was created by someone else in your life. This will surely cause you to want to blame them for this predicament. But to God, it doesn't really matter who created the valley because He's not looking for someone to blame. No matter who created the situation that you find yourself in, God can and will use it to make you stronger.

Take a quick look at The Lord's Prayer. Did you ever notice that right after Jesus gave us that awesome example of prayer, He went back to the part about forgiving others? I believe He merely went back to an extremely important Christian concept – forgiveness; the fact that if I want to be forgiven, I must forgive others.

PRAYER: Lord, today I realize that part of the reason I am in this valley is because of my response to someone else's sin against me. Lord, I choose to forgive them for this because it's the right thing to do, but also because You said in Your Word that I must forgive others if I want to be forgiven; and Lord, You KNOW I want forgiveness.

So today, by choice, I forgive _____and I choose not to hold that sin against them. Help me, Lord, to make this concept of forgiving others a major part of my walk with You. Thank You, Lord for forgiving me; help me to pass along the favor to others.

A Moment of Personal Reflection . . . .

We can travel a path for years blaming someone for the injury we have suffered. Do you carry hurt around with you every day? Is there someone's face that you see first thing in the morning when you awaken to a new day? Why not decide to just let it go; to choose to forgive anyone who has hurt you, whether they intended to or not. And if it's just too hard or the injury is just too deep, ask God to help you let it go. He will – He did it for me.

_____

_____

_____

_____

_____

_____

_____

Mark 11:25 (KJV)
25 *And when ye stand praying, forgive, if ye have ought against any: that your Father also which is in heaven may forgive you your trespasses.*

DAY 4: I THINK I CREATED MY OWN VALLEY!

1 John 1:9 (KJV)
If we confess our sins, he is faithful and just to forgive us our sins, and to cleanse us from all unrighteousness.

Is this a valley of your own creation? Was there something you did or didn't do that actually created this difficult and depressing situation in the first place? Then God wants you to find grace in your valley; to know that even if our own actions cause us to make decisions that create valleys in our Christian walk, we can still know that His love for us didn't change; and that He is still there to help us while we're in the valley, even though this particular valley may be one of our own creation. You see, there really is "no condemnation to those who are in Christ Jesus" (Romans 8:1).

PRAYER: Lord, I did this! I realize that my own actions created this low place in my life. If someone else had been the cause of my valley, it would have been much easier to get past it; I can forgive someone else much more easily than I can forgive myself.

But Lord, You shed Your Blood for me, too. Even after I have walked faithfully with You for years, I can still do it wrong, and I have – many times. But Your forgiveness is still available, so I choose to receive it, Lord. Thank You for Your grace. I choose, today, to receive the forgiveness You freely offer. Thank You, Jesus.

A Moment of Personal Reflection . . . .

It really helps to just admit it; you're not perfect; as a matter of fact, you're far from perfect. Next, the best thing you can do for your life if you're the one who messed it up is to do what you would do for someone else if they messed your life up – forgive. Release yourself from the guilt of what you did and receive what Jesus did for you. Then thank God for His grace.

_____

_____

_____

_____

_____

_____

_____

_____

Hebrews 4:15-16 _(KJV)_
15 For we have not an high priest which cannot be touched with the feeling of our infirmities; but was in all points tempted like as we are, yet without sin. 16 Let us therefore come boldly unto the throne of grace, that we may obtain mercy, and find grace to help in time of need.

1 Peter 4:12-13
The Message

12-13 Friends, when life gets really difficult, don't jump to the conclusion that God isn't on the job. Instead, be glad that you are in the very thick of what Christ experienced. This is a spiritual refining process, with glory just around the corner.

"In God's economy, you must go down into the valley of grief before you can scale the heights of spiritual glory. You must become tired and weary of living alone before you seek and find the fellowship of Christ. You must come to the end of self before you begin to live."

©2016 Billy Graham Evangelistic Association.
Used with permission. All rights reserved.

DAY 5: I DON'T WANT TO BE IN THIS VALLEY!

Psalm 139:1-3 (KJV)
O lord, thou hast searched me, and known me. ²Thou knowest my downsitting and mine uprising, thou understandest my thought afar off. ³Thou compassest my path and my lying down, and art acquainted with all my ways.

As we go through those valleys in life, we find ourselves rejecting any place in life where we are uncomfortable. But it's those uncomfortable places where we learn the most about ourselves and even about God. While we're in that place, though, sometimes we gripe, complain and whine. Why doesn't God move in this situation faster?, we think. And why did God allow it to happen in the first place? Isn't He God? Doesn't He know how much He needs me in ministry somewhere? And doesn't He know that He needs me at my best, not under such a load of heaviness? The answer is, "Yes! He knows!"

Sometimes God refuses to help us out of a valley because there is a higher purpose for where we are; there are things that God desires to teach us in that place; things that we can *only* learn in that miserable valley. As Christians, God wants us to trust Him, no matter how the circumstances appear; no matter how uncomfortable; no matter how distant He seems to be; for Jesus paid the ultimate price for us and He is very much aware of what is going on in the lives of us, His investment!

PRAYER: Dear Lord, this is such a tight, uncomfortable place in which I have found myself. I cry and pray and cry some more and still, no answer. But Lord, I choose to trust You; I choose to turn my focus to Your goodness; Your grace, and Your Plan for my life, no matter what my logic may tell me. I love you, Lord; and I believe; please help my unbelief.

A Moment of Personal Reflection . . . .

It's human nature to want to find a quick exit from an uncomfortable situation. But what if God has a very important lesson for you to learn there? What if the lesson you learn there is one that could have only been learned in that way in that place at that time? Will it not be worth all the trouble when you can look into the eyes of someone that you would love to help and realize that you found their answer in your own valley experience? What natural inclinations will you need to overcome in order to be able to allow yourself to rest in Jesus?

_____

_____

_____

_____

_____

_____

_____

1 Thessalonians 5:18 (KJV)
18 In every thing give thanks: for this is the will of God in Christ Jesus concerning you.

DAY 6: "DON'T BE AFRAID OF THE VALLEY"

Isaiah 41:10 *(KJV)*

10 Fear thou not; for I am with thee: be not dismayed; for I am thy God: I will strengthen thee; yea, I will help thee; yea, I will uphold thee with the right hand of my righteousness.

The next thing I heard the Holy Spirit say to me on that life-changing day at the altar was, "Don't be afraid of your valley." I could hardly think straight. I had, for several months as a teacher in my high school math classroom, had an extremely difficult time remembering student names, much worse than ever before. Sometimes on my way to work as I was getting closer to the railroad tracks where I should turn left to continue to work, I completely forgot which way to turn – and I had taken this route to work for many years.

God was now telling me not to be afraid of this valley? I was terrified! I felt as if I was going crazy. For all I knew, I could have had a tumor or something. But I knew that I had heard the Holy Spirit speaking to me and I have made it my practice, especially over the past few years to just accept what He was saying as the absolute truth and to trust Him. So I told Him, "Okay."

PRAYER: Dear Lord, if I were to be completely honest, I'm terrified about what's happening in my life right now. But I know that You love me with great passion. So, Lord, I choose to trust You with the details of the why's and the when's of my life. I don't know 'why' things are going the way they are and I don't know 'when' that will change, but You do, Lord. I cast the care of my valley situation on You, and I receive Your comfort and love.

16

A Moment of Personal Reflection . . . .

Fear paralyzes you; it keeps you from daring to move in a positive direction. But if you can trust God with childlike faith – like a child with their hand in the hand of someone they trust – you can go through anything. Is there something in your life that has paralyzed you with fear? Write down a statement of faith about your knowledge of God's Presence with you, even in that particular situation. Then thank Him for His Presence and "Fear Not."

_____

_____

_____

_____

_____

_____

_____

_____

1 John 4:18 (KJV)
18 There is no fear in love; but perfect love casteth out fear: because fear hath torment. He that feareth is not made perfect in love.

DAY 7: OPEN YOUR EYES WHILE YOU'RE IN THE VALLEY

1 John 4:9 *(KJV)*
9 In this was manifested the love of God toward us, because that God sent his only begotten Son into the world, that we might live through him.

We tend to just want to get past the valley. It's uncomfortable, even humiliating and we just want the tough stuff to go away. But God would have us to open our eyes while we're in the valleys of life; to take a look around at the things in our lives that drag us down and see His Hand at work in each of them – and to even thank Him for His gracious blessing on even the toughest of situations.

If you're praying for a loved one who is away from God, He wants you to thank Him for what He IS doing in drawing that loved one to the cross; if you're praying for healing for yourself or someone else, God wants you to thank Him for the provision of healing when He shed His precious Blood; if there is a need that you are asking God to meet, whatever the need, it is met in Christ. Don't be afraid; open your eyes in your valley and let the Holy Spirit reassure you that God is right up in the middle of all of the heavy things there.

PRAYER: Lord Jesus, this valley I am in is so comfortable. But Lord, I know that You really are good all the time; and that you are working all things together for my good. Lord, help me not to be afraid to look around while I'm in the valley. Help me to trust You with every single thing that is in my valley. And remind me often, Lord, that You gave Your life so that I could have real life. I still love You, Lord, even as I look at all of the unchanging things in my valley. And I trust You, Lord, with those things and with my own life.

A Moment of Personal Reflection . . . .

I believe that just as we can have childlike faith, we can have childlike fear; fear that causes us to want to crawl under something and hide when we are afraid.

But God would rather have us open our eyes while we are in those valley situations; to take a look at every single fearful thing in our valley and know that He is with us right there in our valley.

What are the specific things or people who are in your valley? Can you 'open your eyes' and look at each of them? Can you hear God's Voice as He reminds you of His Presence with you even here? Write down your thoughts concerning this; choose to trust Him today.

_____

_____

_____

_____

_____

_____

_____

Exodus 33:14 (KJV)
14 *And he said, My presence shall go with thee, and I will give thee rest.*

19

DAY 8: GIVE IT UP! GIVE IT *ALL* UP!

Romans 15:13 *(KJV)*

13 Now the God of hope fill you with all joy and peace in believing, that ye may abound in hope, through the power of the Holy Ghost.

There were things in my life that I was holding onto too tightly and God asked me to give them up to Him and His care: my job or possible lack of one in the future, my hope to get back to the jail and rehab ministries that I dearly loved; my sons and my wishes for their futures. But God's Presence was so real and so addictive that I was willing to give up whatever He asked of me, just as long as I could keep that Precious Peace in my life.

You see, when I held these things so tightly, they became extremely important to me; Well, actually they became *too* important to me. I had forgotten to WHOM I belong. He is the best Father ever and He knows very well how to take care of His Children. I was full of fear: fear of loss; fear of change; and even fear of death.

So, God had gotten me to the place where I wanted to do whatever He asked me to do; and on *this* day, when I heard His Voice, I found myself desperately wanting to do whatever He asked of me; His Presence was so real and so inviting and so invigorating that I felt compelled to do whatever He said – ANYTHING to please Him.

PRAYER: Lord, there is nothing in my life that should be as important to me as You are; *nothing*! Sometimes, though, I don't realize how important certain people and things have become to me until you show me. No person, job or even ministry in my life, Lord, should be more important to me than You are; And there should be nothing that I hope for that, if it were denied, would keep me from loving You and living for You. Help me to keep You in Your rightful place in my heart and in my life.

A Moment of Personal Reflection . . . .

Are there things – or people – in your life that are *too* important to you? Do you, like me, sometimes find yourself holding those things or people too close, as if they are your security blanket?

If you want peace, you must do as God asked me to do; you must give those things and people up. It's a very difficult thing to be asked to do, but the peace that God will give you when you *truly* give up things that are too important to you cannot be compared with any other peace in your life. List below the things and/or people that are too important to you. Pray, giving them to God. Then receive the peace that He alone can give.

_____

_____

_____

_____

_____

_____

_____

Psalm 55:22 (KJV)
22 *Cast thy burden upon the LORD, and he shall sustain thee: he shall never suffer the righteous to be moved.*

21

2 Corinthians 1:3-5
The Message

3-5 **All praise to the God and Father of our Master, Jesus the Messiah! Father of all mercy! God of all healing counsel! He comes alongside us when we go through hard times, and before you know it, he brings us alongside someone else who is going through hard times so that we can be there for that person just as God was there for us. We have plenty of hard times that come from following the Messiah, but no more so than the good times of his healing comfort—we get a full measure of that, too.**

"Just because what's going on in your life right now doesn't feel good doesn't mean God's not working."

JOYCE MEYER
Twitter quote and May 14, 2014
Facebook post, Joyce Meyer
Ministries

DAY 9: DEPRESSION, GONE!!!

Philippians 4:6,7 (KJV)

⁶ Be careful for nothing; but in everything by prayer and supplication with thanksgiving let your requests be made known unto God. ⁷ And the peace of God, which passeth all understanding, shall keep your hearts and minds through Christ Jesus.

I didn't realize how heavy the depression was that was on my life until it was gone! As soon as I 'gave up' everything that the Holy Spirit required me to give up, great peace was mine. As Christians, sometimes we just settle for where we are at the time. However, Jesus bought our peace of mind.

We have a little Pekingese Chihuahua named Choco. He doesn't get table food except when we finish eating, we might let him lick the plate. That's all he knows. He's never been given a whole piece of anything concerning table food so he doesn't know that it exists. To him, it's quite a treat just to get to lick a plate.

But how many of us are just settling for a spiritual 'snack.' We call what we have, "peace" but we are still living with much anxiety. Jesus bought our peace of mind and healing with His Precious Blood. But we just get accustomed to the pain, sickness or anxiety and never go after what Jesus paid for – complete and total healing, physically and mentally.

PRAYER: Lord, there is so much available to me In Christ! But so many times, I settle for a spiritual 'snack' rather than bask in Your peace and in Your Presence. I walk around day after day with an anxious heart and mind. Lord, I want that to change! Help me, Jesus, to receive Your peace more quickly; Help me, Lord, to take more time for You, the Lord of my Life!

A Moment of Personal Reflection . . . .

Is it possible that you are settling for a counterfeit peace? Jesus is your Prince of Peace and He paid a terrific price for your peace.

Write a personal prayer today giving God your anxiety-filled issues. Receive the peace He paid with His Precious Blood for you to have.

_____

_____

_____

_____

_____

_____

_____

_____

John 14:27 (KJV)
27 Peace I leave with you, my peace I give unto you: not as the world giveth, give I unto you. Let not your heart be troubled, neither let it be afraid.

DAY 10: SURELY *THAT* WASN'T GOD!

Psalm 25:4 *(KJV)*
4 Shew me thy ways, O LORD; teach me thy paths.

I thought for sure that the next thing I heard the Holy Spirit say to me couldn't have been God at all. What I thought I heard Him say was, "For a short period of time, I'm allowing even the seizure medication you're taking to purposefully take you further into this valley. But when you come out of this valley, because of this moment, you will be able to identify with and spiritually help more people."

My doctor had been trying to regulate the seizure activity in my brain; so she put me on a new medication for that. For a short period of time, just as God had told me, I felt as if I was going crazy. I stopped several times, as I walked down  the hall in my home and just wept; as I washed dishes, I wept; I got up from sleep many times, went to the den, sat down and just wept uncontrollably.

During all of this, though, I could hear the Holy Spirit so much clearer than before; and I sensed more clearly the love that God has for all of us. So, although I absolutely did not want to be in this low place in my life, that very place was where I found what I had been looking for all along; a place of peace and even contentment.

PRAYER: Dear Lord, I choose to trust You, even when I really don't understand what You are doing in my life or where You are taking me. But Lord, if I can learn more of Your ways; if this valley can enable me to be a more useful tool in Your kingdom, then that is what I want. Wrap Your Arms around me, Lord, and hold me together when I can't seem to find a place of peace. Thank You, Lord, for daring to use me, as frail as I am sometimes.

A Moment of Personal Reflection . . . .

Just like you have your way of doing things, God has HIS way of doing things; and most of the time, His way is amazing, unpredictable, and sometimes hilarious. All He wants from us is faith; All He needs us to do is to believe Him – believe that He can do the impossible and then wait expectantly for Him to do just that.

Is there a situation in your life in which you *must* have a miracle or . . . . you don't even want to think about what might come next? Take a moment and write down your situation in as much detail as you can. Then write your prayer of trust in God for your miracle.

_____

_____

_____

_____

_____

_____

_____

Psalm 28:7 (KJV)
7 *The LORD is my strength and my shield; my heart trusted in him, and I am helped: therefore my heart greatly rejoiceth; and with my song will I praise him.*

DAY 11: GOD'S EXPECTATIONS IN THE VALLEY

Psalm 91:15 (KJV)
He shall call upon me, and I will answer him: I will be with him in trouble; I will deliver him, and honour him.

You see, when we have walked with the Lord for a long time; when we have invested a great percentage of our lives as Christians serving our Lord, He knows what He has created and even perfected in us and He simply will not baby us because He knows what HE has invested in US!
He knows that what He has done in our hearts; what He has taught us is enough; enough to enable us to get through that valley ahead of us. God doesn't grow wimps; He grows men and women who, after serving Him faithfully for many years, are well able, with His help, to handle whatever life hands us and He expects us to handle life's situations by leaning on Him every inch of the way.

PRAYER: Lord, I know I can do better than this; I've been whiny and pitiful. Yes, I've been going through an extremely difficult time, but Your Love for me has never changed. Your help is available for me twenty-four hours a day, seven days a week. I know better.
Remind me, Lord, in times like this, how many times You have brought me through seemingly impossible situations. You have promised never to leave me. So Lord, I depend completely on You. Forgive me for doubting You; and thank You for always being there for me.

A Moment of Personal Reflection . . . .

How long have you known the Lord? Years? Do you think that you've known Him long enough for Him to have expectations of you as His child?

Remember, there really is no condemnation to those who are in Christ Jesus (Romans 8:1). The Lord doesn't condemn you; He's trying to help you to be all that He created you to be. But He will not baby His older children. Think about any areas in your life in which you know that you could do better. Then write a prayer asking for God's help to be all He created you to be.

_____

_____

_____

_____

_____

_____

_____

Luke 18:7-8 (KJV)
7 And shall not God avenge his own elect, which cry day and night unto him, though he bear long with them? 8 I tell you that he will avenge them speedily. Nevertheless when the Son of man cometh, shall he find faith on the earth?

DAY 12: REST IN THE VALLEY

Matthew 11:28,29 (KJV)

28 Come unto me, all ye that labour and are heavy laden, and I will give you rest. 29 Take my yoke upon you, and learn of me; for I am meek and lowly in heart: and ye shall find rest unto your souls.

Are *you* going through a valley right now? Have you found yourself, like me, just wishing that it would all go away? But what if there is something that you can learn in this valley; something that will help someone else? I believe God is asking you, then, to do what He asked me to do: to stop cursing your valley. Instead, He would have you and me to settle down and even *rest* in the valley. Yes, I said rest – in the valley you are in right now. If you belong to Jesus; if you have asked Him into your life, to forgive your sins and make you a new creation; then He did – and He is! He is working in our behalf according to the passion that the Blood of Jesus bought. We can rest in that fact.

But our salvation is not just for us; it's for others. When I am going through a tough time, someone else helps me up; and when that person is going through a tough time, I may help them up. But if, while we are in the valleys of life, we learn nothing, then we have nothing to offer our brother or sister in Christ when they are going through similar circumstances. As I've said: we Americans are very selfish people.

PRAYER: Lord Jesus, I have been so restless and anxious, desperately desiring to get past an uncomfortable situation in my life, in my valley. Help me, Lord, to rest in You; to know that You've got me and You're working Your plan even here, even now. I trust You, Lord. Have Your way in my life.

A Moment of Personal Reflection . . . .

It's hard to admit, but we all know that tough times make us stronger if we lean on Jesus and trust our relationship with Him during our most difficult moments.

Can you cast your care on Him today; not just sort of toss it to Him, but *cast* it on Him with an "I really mean it, Lord" attitude behind it? If you can, and if you *do,* you will experience an amazing peace. You may have to continue to cast that care, but the more you do, the easier it will get. Take a moment and write down your care; then write a prayer to God – a prayer in which you *cast* that care on Him.

_____

_____

_____

_____

_____

_____

1 Peter 5:6-7 (KJV)
6 Humble yourselves therefore under the mighty hand of God, that he may exalt you in due time: 7 Casting all your care upon him; for he careth for you.

Matthew 11:28-30
The Message

28-30 "Are you tired? Worn out? Burned out on religion? Come to me. Get away with me and you'll recover your life. I'll show you how to take a real rest. Walk with me and work with me—watch how I do it. Learn the unforced rhythms of grace. I won't lay anything heavy or ill-fitting on you. Keep company with me and you'll learn to live freely and lightly."

Your Father wants you living life carefree, enjoying His love and knowing that He watches over you. He really loves you. And perfect love – knowing this perfect love – will cast out every fear in your life (1 John 4:18).

From the Joseph Prince Message, "Grace Flows in Worry-Free Areas of Your Life" preached by him on February 17, 2006

DAY 13: I'LL BE ABLE TO REST WHEN.......

Hebrews 4:9 (KJV)
⁹ There remaineth therefore a rest to the people of God.

If anyone in the world ought to be able to have peace in life, it ought to be the Children of God! But how many of us go through our days just as stressed as the rest of the world?

We have plans to rest.....at the end of our work day; or when we have a certain amount of money or when we have the house cleaned up or newly furnished or renovated. But there is a 'rest' that is spoken of in the Book of Hebrews and I believe it is rest that we, as Children of God, can have all day long, no matter what we are doing or where we are going or what we are going through; there is a peace we should have throughout our day.

Rest in your relationship with God through Jesus His Son; rest knowing that He's got you and all of your cares – that is, if you have cast them on Him. Then you will be able to rest no matter where you are.

PRAYER: Dear Lord Jesus, what am I doing? I rush around every day doing what I feel is so necessary – working so that at the end of the day, I can rest. But Lord, I would so love to rest inside all day long, no matter what I am doing; I would love to be able to rest in my relationship with You to the point that I worry about nothing; to not feel the necessity to try to get to a place of 'rest' because the peace that I have is the rest that I seek. Help me, Jesus, to find that rest in my relationship with You that You bought for me with Your Precious Blood! Thank You, Lord, for such a precious gift of rest and peace.

A Moment of Personal Reflection . . . .

Is there something in your life that creates unrest? Can you give that thing to Jesus today; that thing that greets you every morning when you awake and is the last thing on your mind when you go to bed at night; that thing that simply will not let you rest? What is it?

If you're not quite ready to completely give it to Him, can you, at the very least, *begin* to think about giving it to God? Or can you possibly tell Him that you're willing to try, with His help, to lay it down, trusting Him with it? Take a minute and write a note to God about how much you are willing to let go of and trust Him with that thing that is overwhelming your life.

_____

_____

_____

_____

_____

_____

Hebrews 4:1 (KJV)
4 Let us therefore fear, lest, a promise being left us of entering into his rest, any of you should seem to come short of it.

DAY 14: IT'S SO UNCOMFORTABLE HERE IN THE VALLEY!

Joshua 1:9 *(KJV)*

9 Have not I commanded thee? Be strong and of a good courage; be not afraid, neither be thou dismayed: for the LORD thy God is with thee whithersoever thou goest.

I didn't realize until I found myself in this place spiritually how badly we Americans want comfort; we simply want to be comfortable wherever we are. We want the perfect temperature year-round, can't stand to wait in line anywhere for more than a few seconds and stoplights just drive us nuts! So when we read in the Word of God that He would have us to 'wait' on Him, that is very difficult for us to do. Wait on the King of the Universe? The One Who said that "a day with the Lord is as a thousand years and a thousand years as a day?" (2 Peter 3:8) Wait on Him???

What we don't realize is that He is the One who is in control of our situation. Too many times I have caught myself thinking that I am in control and that I want God to help me in my life. But the truth is that I am the *created* being and that the One who created me is the One who is in control of my life and my situation.

Is it possible to find such a place of peace in our relationship with God that we rest, *even* in the valley? I believe so. I believe that this is the Rest spoken of as the Secret Place in Psalm 91. There really is a place in the valley where we can completely rest in Jesus.

PRAYER: Lord, even though I really do appreciate the comforts of life you have given me, sometimes being comfortable actually becomes my goal in life. But that place of eternal comfort is called 'heaven.' So please help me, Lord, to seek to find my rest in my relationship with You and not in the comforts of this life.

A Moment of Personal Reflection . . . .

Is it possible that what you're really craving every day is peace? Is it also possible that you have equated 'peace' with time at the end of the day to physically rest? Ask God today to help you find moments of mental rest; of peace while you work, peace as you drive home, peace as you do whatever you do when you get home from work; peace while you tend to the kids or mow the lawn or........you fill in the blank.

_____

_____

_____

_____

_____

_____

_____

_____

Psalm 91:1-2 (KJV)
91 He that dwelleth in the secret place of the most High shall abide under the shadow of the Almighty. 2 I will say of the LORD, He is my refuge and my fortress: my God; in him will I trust.

DAY 15: THERE IS A PURPOSE FOR THE VALLEY

Ephesians 3:20,21 (KJV)
20 Now unto him that is able to do exceeding abundantly above all that we ask or think, according to the power that worketh in us,
21 Unto him be glory in the church by Christ Jesus throughout all ages, world without end. Amen.

Time in the valley settles things. During that waiting time, God wants to show us where we've been putting Him in our daily walk and where He needs to be; and then He helps us to begin to do that – put Him in His rightful place in our lives – with no condemnation for doing it all wrong!

If we just plead with God to help us to get through that valley as quickly as we can, we miss the whole point of the valley in the first place. God doesn't just allow us to go through a difficult time for no reason. He has a purpose and a plan. The things that He teaches us in the valley will come in very handy when we're faced with someone who is going through a similar valley; and we will find ourselves so thankful to have a word of encouragement that can also help them through their valley.

If we choose to just whimper and cry while we are in the valley, then all that valley serves to do is to make us, our families, and those we encounter miserable. .But the valley can be a quiet place of reflection; a place where we can hear the voice of God more clearly.

PRAYER: God, I never really thought about it that way; that You have a purpose for my going through the valleys of life. But it makes great sense that the most awesome Father in the world would have a purpose and a plan for my life. Thank You, Lord, for Your great love for me – love that will even lead me into a valley!

A Moment of Personal Reflection . . . .

Do you think that maybe you've underestimated God? We all have, of course! Do you honestly think that He would allow you to go through something that has no purpose except to make you miserable?

Write a note to your Heavenly Father today; a letter in which you acknowledge His ability to take care of His child – YOU!

_____

_____

_____

_____

_____

_____

_____

_____

_____

Psalm 23:3 (KJV)
3 He restoreth my soul: he leadeth me in the paths of righteousness for his name's sake.

DAY 16: DON'T RUSH THROUGH YOUR VALLEY

Psalm 139:1-4 (KJV)

139 *O Lord, thou hast searched me, and known me. ² Thou knowest my downsitting and mine uprising, thou understandest my thought afar off. ³ Thou compassest my path and my lying down, and art acquainted with all my ways. ⁴ For there is not a word in my tongue, but, lo, O Lord, thou knowest it altogether.*

Rushing through a valley in life is like trying to rush a cake. It's not done until it's *done*; and there's no need in thinking we can speed up the process, whether we're talking about a cake or a spiritual valley. God's in control when we know Jesus and when it's time for us to begin to come out of the valley, He will begin the process of walking us out of it. We, each of us, have a personal relationship with God through His Son, Jesus. There really is no such thing as 'cookie cutter' Christians. Yes, there are basic commandments and laws that God expects all of us to abide by, but the specifics about how long the process will take through our low points in life is between each of us and Him – in our own relationship with Him. It's personal – very personal.

PRAYER: Lord Jesus, sometimes I think I live in "Stress City!" I find myself so anxious to just get past this stress-filled valley. But Lord, if there is some good that can come from this place, either for me or someone else, then Lord, help me not to rush through this place, as uncomfortable as it is. When I am anxious, Lord, please wrap Your Arms around me and help me to rest in You. Thank You, my Prince of Peace.

A Moment of Personal Reflection . . . .

Do you find yourself, as the rest of us do, wanting to get past this thing, this valley in your life? Does it consume your time and your mind, stealing your peace? God has a purpose for this uncomfortable place you've found yourself in. Can you write a quick note to the Lord, giving Him your anxieties about your situation? Do that today; then ask Him to help you hear His Voice as He teaches you what He wants you to learn in this place in your life.

_____

_____

_____

_____

_____

_____

_____

_____

John 10:27 *(KJV)*
27 My sheep hear my voice, and I know them, and they follow me:

Romans 5:3-5
The Message

3-5 There's more to come: We continue to shout our praise even when we're hemmed in with troubles, because we know how troubles can develop passionate patience in us, and how that patience in turn forges the tempered steel of virtue, keeping us alert for whatever God will do next. In alert expectancy such as this, we're never left feeling shortchanged. Quite the contrary—we can't round up enough containers to hold everything God generously pours into our lives through the Holy Spirit!

"It's painful, but you must allow God to break your stubborn will. If you want your future to be filled with His Presence and His Power, you must hunger and thirst after righteousness like a starving man craving food."

John Hagee Ministries
From a JHM Facebook post
June 1, 2016

DAY 17: IT'S NOT ALL ABOUT ME!

Philippians 2:3 *(KJV)*
3 Let nothing be done through strife or vainglory; but in lowliness of mind let each esteem other better than themselves.

We Americans are so selfish. We've been taught that we only need to consider our own wants; to look out for "number one" and "it's all about me!" But as Christians, we are taught that our lives are to be spent for others. Remember: "Jesus, Others and then Yourself?" This seems to make a great Children's Sunday School lesson, but how many of us as Christian adults practice that kind of "J-O-Y" that we were taught as children?

In the valleys of life, if we're listening, God will direct our attention to others and their needs first. Many scriptures talk about giving and sacrifice; none talk about "looking out for number ONE." When we go through those tough times that are sometimes referred to as valleys, God gives us tools that will enable us to minister to others who are in the same shoes; the same desperate circumstances, but depending on the same faithful God.

PRAYER: Lord Jesus, I find myself thinking so much about my own world, my own needs and wants. But Lord, it's not all about me. I understand that the things that you either direct me to do or allow me to go through in life are not ultimately about me and my comfort; that You also will direct me through very uncomfortable situations so that when I come through my valley, I will be more sensitive to the needs of others; and that, if I am sensitive to Your Spirit as I go through the valley, I will have become equipped to help others who are going through a similar valley. Help me, Lord, to follow Your direction through my valley so that I may be a more useful tool in Your Toolbox!

A Moment of Personal Reflection . . . .

God has a purpose for this uncomfortable place you have found yourself in; and it's not all about you. There are people who are watching how you handle yourself while you're in this valley. They wonder how you can still put on a smile and keep going; and some of them surely would love to talk to you about *their* valley, too. Listen for the Voice of the Holy Spirit as He turns your attention away from your own needs to the needs of others. Write a prayer to God, asking Him to help you to be more sensitive to others while you're in this place in your life.

_____

_____

_____

_____

_____

_____

_____

Philippians 2:4 *(KJV)*
4 Look not every man on his own things, but every man also on the things of others.

DAY 18: WHAT IF?

1 Peter 1:7 (KJV)

7 That the trial of your faith, being much more precious than of gold that perisheth, though it be tried with fire, might be found unto praise and honour and glory at the appearing of Jesus Christ:

In order to move out of my valley, I have to trust God with my "What If" questions. You know, that's the ones that are so full of fear; the questions that keep me from moving forward in my relationship with God; the ones that I wouldn't dare say out loud, but are constantly on my mind.

God wants me to trust Him. Period. Trust Him when things are going well and I realize my blessings come from Him; trust Him when I ask a questions that seem to fall on deaf Ears – even though I know He gave the ultimate price so that He could be in charge of my life and everything that concerns me.

So no matter my "What-If" questions, God's got me and He's got my questions and the answers that go with them. I choose to trust Him!

PRAYER: Lord Jesus, fear has undoubtedly paralyzed me again! Those "What-if" questions are overwhelming my mind. But Lord, I know that You are ultimately in charge of the details of my life. So I choose to trust You and Your great love for me. I resist that spirit of fear in Jesus' Name and I receive Your peace in its place.

Lord, I put my situation in your hands and I trust You with all the details, knowing that You are my great High Priest and that You always live to make intercession for me (Hebrews 7:25). Thank You, Jesus!

A Moment of Personal Reflection . . . .

Do you have any "What If" questions? Resist that spirit of fear and receive the peace that only our Prince of Peace can give you. Ask God to help you move past this paralyzing place called, "What If" and to move on to a more peace-filled walk of faith. There is still no condemnation to those who are in Christ Jesus (Romans 8:1), but receiving God's peace can make difficult places more bearable and help us to bear more fruit in God's Kingdom.

_____

_____

_____

_____

_____

_____

_____

_____

Romans 8:1 *(KJV)*
8 *There is therefore now no condemnation to them which are in Christ Jesus;*

DAY 19: TRUSTING GOD IN THE VALLEY

Proverbs 3:5,6

5 Trust in the LORD with all thine heart; and lean not unto thine own understanding. 6 In all thy ways acknowledge him, and he shall direct thy paths.

This has always been a comforting scripture to my heart, but when I go through the valleys of life, this scripture comes alive to me. When my mind is overwhelmed with 'what could happen' or 'how am I going to ever find peace in this situation,' I must trust God without trying to figure out how He might do what I know He can do. I don't have to know how He does it, I just have to believe that *somehow* He *can* and that He *will*. And then, wherever I am in my day when that situation comes to mind, I acknowledge Him and my own trust in Him, as today's scripture says; and He *will* direct my paths.

PRAYER: Lord, I can't see what You're doing while I'm in this valley; but Your Word assures me that if I will trust You with all my heart; that if I will trust You to the point that I stop trying to figure it all out; that You will direct my path. I understand, Lord, that I can either wring my hands and worry over difficult situations or I can trust You. I choose to trust You. Remind me, Lord, when I am anxious that you are busy at work in my behalf; working 'all things together for my good;' that even THIS most recent thing in my life will work together with other things to bring about something good. Thank You, Lord.

A Moment of Personal Reflection . . . .

Do you have a hard time trusting people? Do you also have a hard time trusting God? It's quite alright to ask the Holy Spirit's help in trusting God, especially in your valley. He is the most trustworthy of anyone in your life. As He reveals areas in your life in which you have a hard time trusting Him, write a note in response to His Call to trust Him in those areas. He really is good.......ALL the time!

_____

_____

_____

_____

_____

_____

_____

_____

_____

Psalm 56:3 *(KJV)*
3 What time I am afraid, I will trust in thee.

DAY 20: I WAS CREATED FOR HIM!

Colossians 1:16 (KJV)
16 For by him were all things created, that are in heaven, and that are in earth, visible and invisible, whether they be thrones, or dominions, or principalities, or powers: all things were created by him, and for him:

What an amazing thought! God created us for His own pleasure; not to boss us around, but for fellowship with Him. Then it must give Him great pleasure when we simply want to talk with Him.

If that is true, can I just be myself when I talk to God? Can I just cry when I need to, ask a question when I need to and just tell Him that I love Him when I want to? Can I sit and read His Word or listen for His Voice sometime? Could that be what we were created to do in the first place?

We were created for Him. So why not spend more time with Him? Why not try to find out what He sees in me; why He loves me so much? Why not receive His great love for me and let it change me from the inside out!

PRAYER: Lord Jesus, I am so humbled that you love me so much. Help me, Lord, to receive that love; to allow it to become part of who I am. Help me, Lord, to let you change me "from glory to glory" by Your Love for me. Then, Lord, maybe I can love others in the same way.

Sometimes I get confused, Lord. Sometimes I act as if the main reason for my existence is for my own life; my own wishes; my own plans. But I understand that I was created for You. So help me, Lord, to be all that You created me to be – for You and for Your Kingdom. In Jesus' Name. Amen!

A Moment of Personal Reflection . . . .

Have you ever had a "What am I here for?" moment; are you having one now? God knew you before you were formed in your mother's womb and had a plan and a purpose for your life. Write a letter thanking God for His Plan for your life. Ask Him to help you trust Him with His awesome Plan!

_____

_____

_____

_____

_____

_____

_____

_____

_____

_____

_____

Jeremiah 1:5 _(KJV)_
5 Before I formed thee in the belly I knew thee;

1 Peter 5:6-7
The Message

6-7 So be content with who you are, and don't put on airs. God's strong hand is on you; he'll promote you at the right time. Live carefree before God; he is most careful with you.

"We are healed to help others.
We are blessed to be a blessing.
We are saved to serve, not to sit around and wait for heaven."

Rick Warren
The Purpose Driven Life
Copyright © 2002, 2011, 2012

DAY 21: WEEPING IN THE VALLEY

Ecclesiastes 3:4 (KJV)
4 A time to weep, and a time to laugh; a time to mourn, and a time to dance;

God doesn't need my weeping and wailing in order to move mountains for me; He needs my faith. He needs me to believe Him; to trust Him; to KNOW that He loves me and that His great love for me is why He will move that mountain – IF He chooses to move that mountain.

No, God doesn't need my weeping in order to change situations; but sometimes *I need* to weep before Him – for *me*. God doesn't need my emotional outcry, but sometimes, in order for me to personally hear Him, or to draw close to Him, *I need* to weep. I need to get that emotional stuff out and not keep it bottled up.

As a matter of fact, the *only* reason I believe He will leave that mountain in my path is if it is *good* for me; if that thing that I am battling is something that I need to overcome; something that I need to win a battle against. In that case, the mountain will only move when I have persevered; it will only move when God says it is time for it to move. After all, He is my Heavenly Father and He's the Best! Not one thing goes unnoticed by my Heavenly Father.

PRAYER: Dear Lord, I am so thankful for Your great love for me. Forgive me, Lord, when I doubt Your love and grumble against Your care. You are an awesome Heavenly Father who takes great care of Your Own. Help me, Lord, to trust You, for You are *always* good.

A Moment of Personal Reflection . . . .

Have you been trying to 'keep it together' but feel like you could explode with emotion? No, God doesn't need your tears, but if you need to cry, then cry. Tears were given to us for a reason. In the space below, talk to God about what's causing any overflow of emotion; give it to Him and trust Him with it.

_____

_____

_____

_____

_____

_____

_____

_____

_____

_____

Colossians 1:17 *(KJV)*
17 And he is before all things, and by him all things consist.

DAY 22: THERE ARE LESSONS THAT CAN *ONLY* BE LEARNED IN THE VALLEY

Isaiah 43:2 (KJV)
² When thou passest through the waters, I will be with thee; and through the rivers, they shall not overflow thee: when thou walkest through the fire, thou shalt not be burned; neither shall the flame kindle upon thee.

Did any of us learn how to drive by watching our parents drive, by reading the driver's manual or by simply studying the car itself? No, we learned to drive by getting behind the steering wheel and maneuvering our way through the twists and turns ahead of us. In the same way, there are some  lessons that can *only* be learned in the low places of our lives; in the places where our faith is tested and tried as we wait on God and trust Him to walk us through extremely difficult places. We cannot learn how to make it through difficult times unless we go *through* them; and we can go through them with *Him*.

PRAYER: Dear Lord, I cringe when I even think about having to go through the valleys of life. But Lord, life here on earth was not easy for You either. So I choose to give myself to whatever You feel that I need to go through in order to be more useful to Your purposes. However, my great consolation, Lord, is that You will be with me no matter what I go through. Thank You, Lord, that You promise never to leave me nor forsake me (Hebrews 13:5).

A Moment of Personal Reflection . . . .

The scripture from Isaiah speaks about passing through the waters and walking through the fire. None of us want to walk through dangerous waters or fire. But it is in those times that we become a sharpened tool for God's use. Are you ready to ask God to help you settle into His Plan for your life? If so, write him a letter telling Him so and honestly asking for His help in becoming what He needs you to be for His Kingdom.

_____

_____

_____

_____

_____

_____

_____

_____

Matthew 28:20 (KJV)
20 Teaching them to observe all things whatsoever I have commanded you: and, lo, I am with you always, even unto the end of the world. Amen.

DAY 23: THANK GOD *FOR* THE VALLEY . . . . REALLY?

2 Corinthians 12:10 *(KJV)*
10 Therefore I take pleasure in infirmities, in reproaches, in necessities, in persecutions, in distresses for Christ's sake: for when I am weak, then am I strong.

Paul had either stumbled upon a very great truth – or he was crazy! How in the world can we take pleasure in any of these situations? They press us down, humiliate us, cause us great pain; they make us feel weak and pitiful.

But Paul had found the "sweet spot" in serving the Lord. He understood that when we go through great discomfort, humiliation, even persecution, we are, at that point in our walk with the Lord, closer to Jesus than at any other time in our lives. In those times, if we allow ourselves, we can gain great insight into the very heart of God and of His Son, Jesus.

PRAYER: Lord, in my uncomfortable situations, those that try my faith, I find myself wanting out as soon as possible! But Lord, I am desperate to know You, to understand what You went through for us, Your Church, and to be of greater value to you in Your Kingdom. Help me, Lord, not to grumble so much in my valley, but to even get to the place where I can be like Paul, the seemingly crazy one who could actually 'take pleasure in" extremely uncomfortable places in life.

A Moment of Personal Reflection . . . .

Have you ever looked into the eyes of someone who was, at that moment in their lives, going through something similar to what you, too, had gone through in your Christian walk? Did you find yourself thankful for having the words of wisdom and encouragement that they needed to hear? Maybe that is what Paul was talking about in today's scripture. Write a quick note thanking God for the blessing you experienced when He used you to encourage that person; then ask Him to do it again!

_____

_____

_____

_____

_____

_____

_____

Matthew 10:8 (KJV)
⁸ *Heal the sick, cleanse the lepers, raise the dead, cast out devils: freely ye have received, freely give.*

DAY 24: WHEN IT'S TIME, GOD WILL WALK YOU OUT OF THE VALLEY

Psalm 23:4 *(KJV)*
4 Yea, though I walk through the valley of the shadow of death, I will fear no evil: for thou art with me; thy rod and thy staff they comfort me.

Throughout scripture, we are spoken of as, "Children of God." Once we are born again, we belong to Him and He is the very best Father and is so keenly aware of our situations – much more than we know within ourselves. He is not like some of our over-bearing parents who put us in tight situations just to watch us squirm. If we are in a tight place, either we have disobeyed God and our own actions have put us there; or we are there expressly for His purpose and to carry out His plan. If we have been disobedient, we need only to get that thing right with Him; but if we know of no disobedience in our lives, we can rest in knowing that the best Father in the world will not leave His child in a place of great discomfort and pain one moment longer than necessary. When God's purpose for the valley is fulfilled, He will walk us right out of that valley!

PRAYER: Father, forgive me when I doubt Your ability to be a 'father' to me. I choose to trust You, God, with every detail of my life, especially the valleys that I must walk through. But I thank You, Father, that when it is time for this valley to be behind me, You will walk me out of it and I will be *better* for having gone through it.

A Moment of Personal Reflection . . . .

Your heavenly Father has a purpose for valley experiences. If you are right in the middle of one of those right now, take hope in knowing that when it is time, God, your Father, will walk you out of the valley. Thank God for that day to come; for it will surely come!

_____

_____

_____

_____

_____

_____

_____

_____

_____

_____

Isaiah 43:11 (KJV)

11 I, even I, am the LORD; and beside me there is no saviour.

Psalm 27:14
King James Version

14 Wait on the LORD: be of good courage, and he shall strengthen thine heart: wait, I say, on the LORD.

"Hope is not that God will deliver you *from* your circumstances.

Hope is that God will help you walk *through* your circumstances."

Robert Morris
Quoted from audio teaching,
"The Prison Test"

DAY 25: MUST FOCUS ON THE POSITIVES; CAN'T FOCUS ON THE NEGATIVES......

2 Corinthians 4:17-18 *(KJV)*

17 For our light affliction, which is but for a moment, worketh for us a far more exceeding and eternal weight of glory; 18 While we look not at the things which are seen, but at the things which are not seen: for the things which are seen are temporal; but the things which are not seen are eternal.

Light affliction? This is no light affliction that I am going through! It's a dark valley full of loneliness and hopelessness. And the Word says that it's 'but for a moment?' Seems like it's already been forever! But it also says that it is working for us a far more exceeding and eternal weight of glory! Whew! Thank You, Jesus.

The next statement in this scripture reference is, "while we look not at the things which are seen, but at the things which are not seen." Okay, so my focus has got to be on something, but it can't be on what I can see; my focus must be on God and His goodness; on His mercy, and especially on His love for me and for those I pray for. God will honor my faith if I will just keep my focus on Him, not on the changing circumstances before me. Help me, Jesus!

PRAYER: Lord, it's so easy to let the negative circumstances capture my attention when I am going through a valley. Help me, Lord, to keep my focus on You especially in those times. Remind me of Your great mercy and grace; that Your amazing love for Your people is what sent you to the cross for us in the first place. Thank You, Jesus!

A Moment of Personal Reflection . . . .

Do your thoughts tend to gravitate toward the negative things that happen in your life rather than the encouragement that scripture brings? We will all experience good and not-so-good times in life. But we can know peace in the middle of our conflicts. Write down a few of those positive reflections that are true every day of your life. Do this often. Then, when extreme difficulties come, it will be easier to turn your thoughts toward the goodness of God and His Word.

_____

_____

_____

_____

_____

_____

_____

Romans 12:2 *(KJV)*
2 And be not conformed to this world: but be ye transformed by the renewing of your mind, that ye may prove what is that good, and acceptable, and perfect, will of God.

DAY 26: WAITING ON . . . . GOD?

Isaiah 40:31 (KJV)

But they that wait upon the LORD shall renew their strength; they shall mount up with wings as eagles; they shall run, and not be weary; and they shall walk, and not faint.

Waiting is uncomfortable. Waiting takes the situation out of my hands and puts it into Someone Else's Hands – God's!

And during those hours of waiting, the Holy Spirit will inspect my heart and show me, without any condemnation, where my heart really is.

For if we, in the valley, really are waiting on the Lord, we will grow stronger; and we, as eagles, will feel the wind of the Holy Spirit as He comes near, informing us that we can, by faith, stretch out our spiritual 'wings' to prepare for the moment when we are ready to come out of our valley, ready to 'fly' in the Name of Jesus!

PRAYER: Help me, Jesus! I get so anxious even though I know you love me with an everlasting love (Jer. 31:3) and are working all things together for my good (Rom. 8:28). It gets so uncomfortable waiting. Teach me, Lord, how to trust You while You work in my behalf. Show me in Your Word how others have waited on You in a way that pleases You. Help me to hear Your Voice as You direct me to take roads that I probably would not have chosen to take on my own. For as You direct, I know that You have a Plan that may not be the most comfortable; but I honestly do want You to use me in whatever capacity You Choose that will bring honor and glory to Your Name. Help Me, Lord!

A Moment of Personal Reflection . . . .

How does the phrase, 'waiting on God' sound to you? On the lines below, write down what exactly that means to you – the positive and the negative connotations. The write down the blessings that can come from a decision to wait on Him.

_____

_____

_____

_____

_____

_____

_____

_____

_____

_____

Psalm 27:14 *(KJV)*
14 Wait on the LORD: be of good courage, and he shall strengthen thine heart: wait, I say, on the LORD.

DAY 27: GOD'S PLAN VERSUS MY PLAN

Jeremiah 29:11 (KJV)
11 For I know the thoughts that I think toward you, saith the LORD, thoughts of peace, and not of evil, to give you an expected end.

Valleys are part of God's Plan for our lives. They produce character. They try our faith and cause us to draw close to God. They cause us to make absolute decisions at some point in our distress; decisions that will stand test after test later.

A valley is where you dig your heels in and persevere until you are through to the other side. God knows what that process will produce in us. He also knows that we would have never, ever chosen to go this way. But the only way that the character of Jesus can be produced in us is through the sufferings of Jesus.

So we find ourselves humbled, feeling alone and even forsaken. We question God as to what kind of good can come from our situation, but we conclude our prayers with, "I trust You, God."

God *knows*, but He doesn't necessarily tell us, the plans that He has for us. Plans to prosper us – prosperity according to God's dictionary is very different from the definition we find in our own dictionaries. God's prosperity produces godly character, faith, perseverance and a trust in Him that cannot be found without going 'through' the valley.

PRAYER: Lord Jesus, I choose to trust You and Your Plans for me. I want to be like You, but I don't know how to do that. So Lord, I give you permission to take charge of my life so that I might produce fruit; so that I might bring honor and glory to Your Name. Thank You, Jesus, for dying for me; help me now to live for You. Amen.

A Moment of Personal Reflection . . . .

Do you ever picture God wringing His hands over you or maybe throwing them up into the air as if He were giving up on you? Write a quick thank-you note to God today, thanking Him for His kind thoughts toward you. Ask Him to help you remember this the next time you or someone else have made a mess of things: God's thoughts toward us, even in those moments, are thoughts of peace; and He has an awesome Plan!

_____

_____

_____

_____

_____

_____

_____

_____

2 Corinthians 12:9 (KJV)
9 *And he said unto me, My grace is sufficient for thee: for my strength is made perfect in weakness. Most gladly therefore will I rather glory in my infirmities, that the power of Christ may rest upon me.*

DAY 28: PAUL'S AMAZING RESPONSE TO HIS VALLEYS

2 Corinthians *12:10* *(KJV)*
¹⁰ Therefore I take pleasure in infirmities, in reproaches, in necessities, in persecutions, in distresses for Christ's sake: for when I am weak, then am I strong.

I'm not anywhere near where Paul was when He wrote this scripture by the inspiration of the Holy Spirit, but I believe we should all be headed in this direction. When we're in a personal valley, the purpose of that valley is to enable us to draw closer to God, sharing in Jesus' sufferings; but it also enables us to identify with those in our world who are hurting and sometimes, to even give them words of encouragement and healing.

"I am NOT upset. I'm just more animated than usual."

My stuff in my world is not just about me; it's about those who will also glean from the wisdom God will give me in my own personal valleys. What a great big God we serve!

PRAYER: Lord, how many times in my valleys do I just lose it emotionally! My thoughts are just on winning an argument or appearing good or right or just better than the other person. But Lord, You taught Paul, and You are teaching us through his writings, that we should remember what Paul was trying to say; that if we'll lean on You and listen to You in the middle of our difficulties, that You will teach us Your way to handle it. Lord, help us also to remember that there is NO – ABSOLUTELY NO condemnation to those who are in Christ Jesus, even when we are in a valley. Thank You, Jesus!

A Moment of Personal Reflection . . . .

You may be like me, thinking how in the world could Paul take pleasure in these extremely negative circumstances. But maybe you and I can at least acknowledge that God is right up in the middle of everything we are going through; and we can take today's scripture from 2 Corinthians, which was penned by Paul (through the inspiration of the Holy Spirit) by faith that says that when we are weak, then we are strong. Write your thoughts about how this can help you in your day-to-day living.

_____

_____

_____

_____

_____

_____

_____

_____

Psalm 73:28 *(KJV)*
28 But it is good for me to draw near to God: I have put my trust in the Lord GOD, that I may declare all thy works.

DAY 29: IDENTIFICATION WITH THE SUFFERINGS OF JESUS IN THE VALLEY

2 Corinthians 1:4 (*KJV*)
4 Who comforteth us in all our tribulation, that we may be able to comfort them which are in any trouble, by the comfort wherewith we ourselves are comforted of God.

It seems that in this experience that God is taking me through, I am realizing that the more I suffer, the more I go through *with* Jesus and not against Him, the more I sense His Presence. Maybe, just maybe when we go through low, depressing times, but without complaining; maybe we find a place of identification with Jesus in suffering. Part of being a Christian is suffering in His Name.

I see the undeniable value of this when I look into the eyes of someone who is going through a deep, depressing place in life. When I have gone through a similar place, I am able to encourage that person with the same encouragement I received from the Lord during my own low place. That's amazing!

PRAYER: Lord, I don't even like myself when I complain! Help me, Jesus, to trust You during those low places, during those valley experiences. And remind me, Lord, that one day You will use the things that you taught me in my valley experience to encourage a brother or sister in Christ. And should I find that place of fellowship with you in suffering, Lord, I will be so honored to cast that crown at your feet in heaven. God, You are such a Big God!!!

A Moment of Personal Reflection . . . .

Does this message grab you like it does me? You've surely seen the movies like I have – the ones where someone has a choice to just get out of a situation or to go through it with their friend. Write a message about what you think it will be like when you see Jesus face to face and you *know* that He is pleased that you chose to suffer for His Name.

_____

_____

_____

_____

_____

_____

_____

_____

1 Peter 5:10 (KJV)
10 But the God of all grace, who hath called us unto his eternal glory by Christ Jesus, after that ye have suffered a while, make you perfect, stablish, strengthen, settle you.

DAY 30: CROWNS OF GLORY TO CAST AT THE FEET OF JESUS – BECAUSE OF THE VALLEY

1 Corinthians 3:11-15 (KJV)

11 For other foundation can no man lay than that is laid, which is Jesus Christ. 12 Now if any man build upon this foundation gold, silver, precious stones, wood, hay, stubble; 13 Every man's work shall be made manifest: for the day shall declare it, because it shall be revealed by fire; and the fire shall try every man's work of what sort it is. 14 If any man's work abide which he hath built thereupon, he shall receive a reward. 15 If any man's work shall be burned, he shall suffer loss: but he himself shall be saved; yet so as by fire.

When it's all over here; when every single person who has ever lived is either in heaven or hell and life as we know it is over, there will be a day when our works are judged and we will receive rewards for those things we did for Jesus.

Do you want to one day stand before God with mere thanksgiving for the things He gave you? Do you want to stand before Him knowing that He brought you through so many difficult times unscathed? Or would you rather stand before Him knowing that you went through extremely difficult times *with Him*, finding the "fellowship of His sufferings" to be a blessing you found in your valley.

PRAYER: Lord Jesus, thank You for Your blessings on my life; but help me, Lord, to humbly walk with You through my valleys, knowing that You are with me through every twist and turn, somehow bringing honor and Glory to Your Name.

A Moment of Personal Reflection . . . .

When this life is over, don't you want to have *something* to give to the One Who 'loved you and gave Himself up for you?' Once we're there with Him, whatever we've done on earth is over. There will be nothing to add to it. Write a final message to Jesus telling Him what you want your 'thank-You' to look like when you finally step from this life into heaven. Then ask His help to bring it to pass.

_____

_____

_____

_____

_____

_____

_____

_____

_____

2 Corinthians 9:8 *(KJV)*
8 And God is able to make all grace abound toward you; that ye, always having all sufficiency in all things, may abound to every good work:

ABOUT THE AUTHOR

Renee` Shipp is a math teacher with ten years teaching experience at the high school and college level. A few years ago, after editing her pastor, Jeff Scurlock's book entitled *The Eye of a Needle*, she began to think about writing a children's book. Using some photographs, she produced her first book, entitled, *Hayden, Papa and the Plum Tree*. From there, she branched out to edit books for people in her community.

Pouring the Word of God into men and women at the local jail and rehab still continues to bring Renee great joy, even after many years. Her next venture will be a book to help the incarcerated and those in rehab deal with the stuff of life in a Christian way.

Renee and her husband of over 30 years, Lawton Shipp, live in East Brewton, Alabama. Their two grown sons, Jay and Greg, along with their only grandson, Hayden, are their pride and joy.

The Shipps are very active in their church, The First Assembly of God in East Brewton, Alabama where her husband has served on the Board for many years and she has been a Sunday School teacher as well. She and her husband sincerely believe that a relationship with God through His Son, Jesus, is the most important and fulfilling relationship anyone can ever have.

Renee` Shipp
Author of *Hayden, Papa and the Plum Tree*
rshippteacher@yahoo.com
On Facebook: Renee Seay Shipp

Made in the USA
Lexington, KY
08 August 2019